BABY SHEEP

by Martha London

Cody Koala
An Imprint of Pop!
popbooksonline.com

abdobooks.com
Published by Pop!, a division of ABDO, PO Box 398166, Minneapolis, Minnesota 55439.

Printed in the United States of America, North Mankato, Minnesota

052020
092020

THIS BOOK CONTAINS RECYCLED MATERIALS

Cover Photo: Shutterstock Images
Interior Photos: Shutterstock Images, 1, 6, 11; iStockphoto, 5 (top), 5 (bottom left), 5 (bottom right), 9, 13 (top), 13 (bottom left), 13 (bottom right), 14, 16–17, 19, 20

Editor: Nick Rebman
Series Designer: Christine Ha

Library of Congress Control Number: 2019955133

Publisher's Cataloging-in-Publication Data
Names: London, Martha, author.
Title: Baby sheep / by Martha London
Description: Minneapolis, Minnesota : POP!, 2021 | Series: Baby farm animals | Includes online resources and index
Identifiers: ISBN 9781532167485 (lib. bdg.) | ISBN 9781532168581 (ebook)
Subjects: LCSH: Sheep--Infancy--Juvenile literature. | Lambs--Juvenile literature. | Baby farm animals--Juvenile literature. | Animal babies--Juvenile literature.
Classification: DDC 636.3--dc23

Hello! My name is

Cody Koala

Pop open this book and you'll find QR codes like this one, loaded with information, so you can learn even more!

Scan this code* and others like it while you read, or visit the website below to make this book pop.

popbooksonline.com/baby-sheep

*Scanning QR codes requires a web-enabled smart device with a QR code reader app and a camera.

Table of Contents

Chapter 1

Little Lamb

Sheep have thick fur. It is called wool. Baby sheep are called lambs. They are **mammals**. When lambs are young, they drink their mothers' milk.

Watch a video here!

Some sheep give birth in fields. But many give birth in barns. The mother sheep and lambs stay inside for a few days. Lambs are less likely to get sick inside a barn.

There are more than 200 kinds of sheep.

Chapter 2

Part of the Flock

Lambs are born with soft wool. They have big ears and short tails. Lambs have **hooves** on their feet. Their hooves are hard.

Learn more here!

Lambs stay close to their mothers. Sheep live in groups called flocks. They stay close to one another. Flocks help sheep stay safe.

eye
ear
wool
tail
hoof

Chapter 3

Growing Up

Lambs try new foods as they get older. They stop drinking milk when they are three months old. They eat solid food instead.

Learn more here!

Sheep **graze** in fields. They eat grass and other plants. A sheep's upper lip is split. The split lip helps the sheep eat grass growing close to the ground.

Some sheep live in apple orchards. They eat weeds but not apples.

A sheep re-chews its food during the day. The food moves through the sheep's

four **stomachs**. This helps the sheep get more **nutrients** from its food.

Chapter 4

Shearing Sheep

Farmers raise sheep for many reasons. Some farmers sell wool. People make clothes out of wool. Lambs that are raised for wool stay with their flock.

Complete an activity here!

Other farmers raise sheep for milk. They sell the milk so people can make cheese. All farmers **shear** their sheep's wool. Shearing does not hurt the sheep.

A sheep's wool never stops growing.

Making Connections

Text-to-Self

If you were a farmer, would you want to have a flock of sheep? Why or why not?

Text-to-Text

What other books have you read about animals that are raised for milk? What animals were they?

Text-to-World

A sheep's wool never stops growing. What might happen if a farmer didn't shear it?

Glossary

graze – to eat grass or other plants in a field.

hooves – the hard parts that cover an animal's feet.

mammal – a type of animal that has hair or fur and feeds milk to its young.

nutrient – part of food that humans, animals, and plants need to stay strong and healthy.

shear – to cut a sheep's wool off its body.

stomach – a body part that takes in food that has been eaten.

Index

Online Resources

popbooksonline.com

Thanks for reading this Cody Koala book!

Scan this code* and others like it in this book, or visit the website below to make this book pop!

popbooksonline.com/baby-sheep

*Scanning QR codes requires a web-enabled smart device with a QR code reader app and a camera.